The Child Within

By

Freda V. Lieb

AmErica House
Baltimore

First printing

ISBN: 1-58851-716-0
PUBLISHED BY AMERICA HOUSE BOOK PUBLISHERS
www.publishamerica.com
Baltimore

Printed in the United States of America

In full consciousness
of mind and spirit,
I acknowledge that
I am only the vessel
through which
God's Holy Spirit
has worked to complete
this collection of poems.

Amen
Blessing and glory and wisdom,
Thanksgiving and honor and power and might,
Be to our God forever and ever.
Amen.
Revelation 7:12

Dedicated to
God the Father, God the Son,
and God the Holy Spirit

The Child Within

The child within,
understood not,
why the door was closed,
why the door was locked,
but the Father came,
in God the Son,
to unlock the door,
to bid the child come,

The Father and child,
going in and out,
'til the child has learned,
to trust the Son,
the Word Perfect,
the picture of life,
in a little child,
with a future bright.

Knowing
There is no peace without forgiveness
no Saving Grace without repentance,
and no real joy without contentment.

A Friend Named Jesus
A friend is as near,
as a loved one so dear,
yet no greater love has been known,
than the love of the one who loved us so,
that He gave us His only Son.

Now Jesus went home to prepare,
and the angels rejoice to hear,
that His friends are as near,
as the loved ones so dear,
who come into that heavenly sphere.

A Golden Harvest

This is indeed the day of the Lord,
as we look upon the golden corn,
almost ready for the reapers, and we see
the richness of the earth and sky,
that makes the seed of our faith grow
deeper still, and as the beauty of the harvest sky,
touches the trees in their glorious hues,
the red, the gold, and the green,
perfectly blending with the tips of the dry leaves,
giving the appearance of shining gemstones,
as the sun brushes them ever so gently,
the same sun that gave the corn it's golden hue,
that gave warmth to the seed planted in springtime past,
to give new life so abundantly, so the harvest truly is
ready,
and as the reapers come for the golden corn, we give
thanks
for the hearts that planted the seed so tenderly.

A Place Called Home
Christ's church is,
a place where God's Grace
and His Mercy abound,
a place where orphans
truly can find a home,
a place where the broken
heart can mend,
and a place where all
spiritual gifts are honed,
most important of all
Christ's church is,
a place where God's Spirit
anchors the soul.

The Pretender
What appears as spiritual, yet is without name,
it resembles life, but remains the same,
in an image being, the most evil of banes.
contemned and innate, pride of his domain.

Where idol-worship is world-renowned,
covered by sin, perverse and blind,
comes then the death of this spiritual mime,
the apostate pretender to God's Throne.

What appears as spiritual has a given name,
the apostate pretender to God's heavenly fame,
from the greatest height, he's the star that fell,
wormwood's his name, pretender of the faith.

Before God's throne, though just for a moment,
Oh rue the time given to this spiritual mime,
a kingdom of demons, a kingdom for souls,
Oh fires of the night, burn forever their blight.

A Time For Throwing Away

Circles and squares and points of white lace,
silk hearts and flowers make perfect finesse,
star-bursts that glow on neon-like snow,
as many cups are raised in joyful conquest.

But nickels and dimes no longer spend,
a dollar won't do and plastic wears thin,
will the rich get richer even in the end,
when money won't buy even a morsel of bread.

A Voice of Hope
At the foot of the cross we weep in sorrow,
at the death of our Lord, how can we face tomorrow,
Jesus, we know that thou did'st promise,
but how can we believe when you are taken from us,
Lord we hear your call, we understand your command,
to help one another and to love our fellow man,
breathe on us your Spirit, Lord, for we cannot alone,
when our sinful nature is left to tend it's own.

But you are always there, Lord,
every where I choose to go,
and you are always there, Lord,
even when I do not know,
and as I look back on the pathway dreaded,
I see the Cross where you died, reviled and rejected,
Oh Lord, your love is ever true,
please strengthen me as I stand for you.

Agape Love
Oh Love, God's Love,
Oh, what Love is born,
the Son of man, yet so much more,

Oh Love, God's Love,
for mortal man to be restored,
the Son of God, in Grace so pure,

Oh Love, God's Love,
made for awhile a little lower,
than the angels that 'round Him hover,

Yet in Glory, the Rock of ages,
the Son of God, most highly favored,
Agape Love transformed and saved us.

Amazing Love
Oh my Lord how you love me,
I cannot count the ways,
from the heights of the heavens,
to the depths of the sea,
for the peace and assurance,
you've given to me,

Oh my Lord how you love me,
how can I ever thank thee,
for the tiny little children,
who play at my knee,
for the food on my table,
for all the beauty I see,

Oh my Lord how you love me,
I think how can this be,
and I bow in awe of thee,
for all of creation is thine to own,
and all I have to give back,
is the love I owe.

Angelic Attire
By God's design, angelic attire,
ministering spirit's of wind and fire,
to pre-empt the serpents line,
to the retaining of believers in Christ,
in perfection, through Christ supplied,
all praise and glory to God Most High.

The Pearly Gates swing open wide,
to receive the last and the first in flight,
in their angelic insignia attire,
for all ages past are now retired,
and to the nations comes now their desire,
in His crowning glory, the coronation of Christ,
and all earth and the heavens reply,
with loud Hosannas to our God Most High.

Angels and People
The Bible tells us in it's pages,
angels have been here throughout the ages,
and though we may be unaware
angels are around us everywhere,
God sends them to help us when we pray,
a friend or a stranger giving strength for the day,
angels are real, I believe it's true,
and that angels are sometimes people too,

Thank you Lord for angels and people,
let this be my petition as I pray,
strengthen me early on my way,
let me be your angel sent to someone each day.

As The Tree Grows
See the tree, how big it's grown,
it's limbs stretch out the world to own,
yet in his heart the devil knows,
that Jesus Christ has sealed his doom,
so even though the tree has grown,
it can't reach up to claim God's throne,
the time grows short and the devil knows,
God will destroy him, and all his own,
he will be cast down to flames of hell,
where the worm dies not in his forever home,
so when you see the tree, how big it's grown,
know that as it grows the end must come.

Assurance

If I must sleep
may my soul find sweet peace,
may my spirit be caught up to heaven,
may my soul find release from the alter beneath,
where all of my sins were forgiven,
and may I find sweet communion,
with Christ's Spirit in union,
at rest from my earthly commission.

Now as I lay me down to sleep,
I will rest in sweet peace,
knowing the assurance I'm given,
for Christ died to save,
Oh 'twas not done in vain,
I know that the Lord my God reigneth.

At The Crossroads
The young men have visions,
the old men dream dreams,
all of these from the Savior, have gleaned,
the young men have seen a great light,
the same light of their father's dream,
and now comes the days fore-told,
when all eyes will look upon,
the light of their visions and dreams.

But as for the sages of the ages who say,
'tis the beginning of a new world age,
as the first light of dawn ushers in the new day,
there at it's portals we can see two gates,
through one we see a vision of heaven,
but through the other one, oh can't you tell,
through the other one we can see no mercy,
for the other gate leads straight into hell.

At The Second Coming
The Christ-Child is gone,
the Deliverer comes,
the mystery is finished,
the last trumpet sounds,
the four winds are gathered,
to call the faithful home,
great is their reward,
when their Savior comes.

But the horror, oh the horror,
count three times the horror,
when the seed of wickedness planted,
bears the fruit of it's evil core,
for upon the earth springs the horror,
whose name is called the destroyer.

Between Shadows and Light
Between shadows and light demonic demons delight,
making weary the traveler on earth's most solemn flight,
into the shadows they wander, the souls that long to rest,
while the demons laugh and taunt as the soldier is put to
the test,

But wait, what victory there, where Jesus the God-Head
lay,
to Christ raise high the victory banner o'er the shadows of
the grave,
to the God-Head, the three in one, to the God-Head, the
victory song,
to the God-Head, raise high the banner, to the God-Head
where the righteous throng.

O, shadows of the night be gone, flee at the first light of
dawn
the true light from heaven come down to judge between
right and wrong,
be still, O, my soul, and wait, for Jesus even now is on the
way,
what glory, what power, what grace, His Righteousness
falls on His saints,

yes, be still O' my soul, and wait, lift up thy voice in
praise,
to Christ the avenger yet pray and you shall not be weary
nor faint.

Rue on Ruse
Rue on Ruse, heartache on heartache,
when the two become one hue,
the scarlet beast, the angel of light,
Lucifer, Satan, the anti-Christ.

Rue on Ruse, heartache on heartache,
when the false prophet and his demons take arms,
to lead astray the world at large,
to destroy the two witness' of Jesus Christ,
but will they succeed against the Day of the Lord,
when Christ returns and God's wrath is poured,
onto all the earth, for God Himself has sworn,
He will not turn back, we have been fore-warned.

But that scarlet beast, the old red dragon,
who with his angels was cast from heaven,
that scourge of man in his hour of power,
leaps from hell's flames, his anger hot to devour,
yet God does not turn aside, nor does He slumber,
His judgments are swifter than the speed of light-bearers,
and the end is near for God Himself has sworn.
He will not turn back, we have been fore-warned.

Rue on Ruse, heartache on heartache,
believe God's Word for there is no other,
and God redeems all those He has favored,
by His Grace and by His shed blood,
all those who believe in God their Savior,
they are Christ's children for God has saved them.

Born For Glory

Silver streaks on golden fleece,
a lamb, a goat, two flocks of sheep,
born for glory and not for loss,
born to die upon a cross,
born to die but not for loss,
engraved for all eternity,
my Savior died to sanctify me.

Born to glory but not for loss,
born to glory in the cross,
silver streaks on golden fleece,
the blood of Christ empowers me,
in the spirit of all prophecy,
through Jesus Christ,
God's Spirit speaks.

Casting Lots
Fire on ice,
out-takes on life,
from winter's glory,
a lack-luster story,
commercial carriers,
desire, not marriage,
freedom intangible,
emotions changeable,
the end of life,
as we know it,
time flies by,
no one can own it,
fire on ice,
reflections of night,
given to desire,
in the mid-night hour,
the melting pot,
is hot, is hot,
betwixt, between,
men cast their lot.

Oh my soul,
do not succumb,
be fire on ice,
be not lukewarm,
in the fullness of time,
when the angels come,
when from my soul,
my spirit has flown,

Oh to hear God say,
to me, "well done",
Oh my soul,
let it be known,
my heart's desire,
be not lukewarm,
be zealous for Christ,
'til my Savior comes,
and, oh my soul,
be not cast down,
there before God's Throne,
I'll cast life's crown.

Closer To Thee
Oh Lord, draw me close and comfort me,
I am terrified of all this evil I see,
the evil that takes men's faith away,
faith that would set all the children free,
Oh Lord, let not this hope fade away,
the hope of those things unseen,
for when hope fades away
in the light of the day,
how dark is that day indeed,
as the darkest night, is the day without hope,
Oh lord, draw me closer to thee,
let no evil find a way to deceive,
the faith in your love that set me free,

Oh Lord, draw me close and comfort me,
you are the Good Shepard who never slumbers nor sleeps,
and you know the way, you won't lead me astray,
Oh Lord, you have loved even me.

Counting My Blessings

I have blessed you and you did not even know,
today I heard my Savior say to me,
don't you see what I have done,
I gave the stars, the moon, and sun,
I have blessed you even though you could not see,

I have blessed you as you watched your children grow,
today I heard my Savior say to me,
O, can't you see what I have done,
I have loved them every one,
so much I also gave my life for these,

I will bless you ever yet with all of these,
today I heard my Savior say to me,
and when you cross to the other shore,
I will bless you even more,
because on Jesus name you have believed,

I have blessed you even though you did not see,
today I heard my Savior say to me,
but now you see what I have done,
that you may live, I gave my Son,
and Jesus' life is now my blessing unto thee,

O, don't you see what He has done,
that you may live God gave His Son,
and Jesus' life is now God's blessing unto thee.

Crystal Clear
The crystal clear river
flows down from on high,
flowing to the depths of life's sea,
it flows to wherever
God's Spirit leads.

The crystal clear river
flows from the high mount,
returning whenever God beckons it to come,
Oh crystal clear river return, return,
return to your home in the clouds

Defining Futility
The futility is in the fertility of make-believe,
on the way to nirvana, is utopia revealed,
in the fallowed soil where man plants the seed,
into the surreal, the futility of man leads,
into the invisible fertility of the make-believe.

Even So, Lord Jesus, Come

I hunger, I thirst, Living God, for thy Word,
Living Water, Living Spirit, come quickly to earth,
Abba Father, Bread of Heaven, rebuke death's wide berth,
Lord Jesus, I yearn, redeemed, I'm secure,
in the Light of thy Word, I want nothing of earth,
for thou hast filled up my cup and I will ever be loved,
no more hunger, no more thirst, no more earth's bitter cup,
let thy righteousness flourish, Holy Spirit quench my
thirst,
let my soul ever praise thee, fill my soul with thy Word,
open wide doors of heaven as thou wilt take me home
as I am filled with thy Spirit, even so, Lord Jesus, come,
open wide the doors of heaven as thou wilt take me home.

Fallen
The great tree of the forest,
is fallen, is fallen,
how great is the noise of it's fall,
uprooted, broken and silenced,
torn from it's place by God,
with it's roots all exposed,
it lays barren and cold,
Oh the great tree of the forest,
suddenly, suddenly is gone,

Lesser trees of the forest,
take notice,
for the gates of hell,
will not prevail,
against the Kingdom of God,
when Christ is revealed.

Feelings

How could I understand another's pain,
if I did not feel it very deep within,
how could I share another's joy,
if I did not feel it very deep within,

How could God understand the trials of men,
if He did not come to dwell among them,
how could I believe Christ lives indeed,
if I did not know it from deep within,

How can I thank the Good Lord above,
for the joy in my heart that comes from Him
and knowing that my Lord forever lives,
brings me great peace from deep within.

Fight or Flight

By God's design, it's fight or flight,
still wrong is wrong and right is right,
but man disdains to light the light,
so he turns his head to run in fright,
sets up his vigil in the long, dark night,
where the wrong becomes the accepted right,
his life is void, he's distracted by his plight,
'til he accepts that truth is light.

Focused
Focus not on past events,
dwell not there on past mistakes,
close not the door to future climbs,
let the past be resigned to doing time,
for focus must become mind-set,
to raise a standard and then perfect,
the future offers it's clean, fresh slate,
giving distance to past mistakes.

Food For Thought
Quickened by God in the middle of the night,
I cannot sleep 'til I rise to write,
with pen in hand, words formed in my mind,
I rise me up early, in the middle of the night.

In the middle of the day, when I think it not,
to pen a line all work must stop,
of food and drink I take no thought,
for when God calls to me, it is enough.

When God calls to me the time is right,
for His words fill me and His gift delights,
for in my head, e'en before I write,
a line formed and a poem is rhymed.

For Whom The Spirit Leads
Strong and lean, a tender young reed,
made to bend with the wind, but not to break,
with a heart to listen, to hear God speak,
in spirit and in truth, God's Will to seek
the watchman does whatever it takes,
and a voice cries out from the wilderness,
from the depths of his being, for whom the spirit leads,
and a voice cries out, repent, repent,
for the Kingdom of God is close at hand,
and the Spirit bids all to enter in.

From Deep Within
Lord, take my sin buried deep within,
Lord, let my heart be fully cleansed,
wash me cleanse me from every stain,
that I may know thy peace again.

Oh Lord, let my soul be white as snow,
for this thy blood doth freely flow,
I pray thee, Oh Lord, my heart to keep,
for 'tis now and forever thy way I seek.

God Blesses Anton
Anton, leave behind you the days of your youth,
for God longs to clothe you in garments of truth,
His blessings extend far beyond hopes and schemes,
that have captured your heart in the land of your dreams,
Eternity is placed in the hearts of all men,
who must then acknowledge that God alone gives,
blessings and honor to whomever He will,
and He blesses all those who believe that He lives.

Anton, God has blessed you, if only you will,
leave behind you the land where your life's-blood was
spilled,
where your youth was used up by another man's will,
for God longs to clothe you in eternal life still,
and now no man may curse what God chooses to bless,
for see, God has blessed you with eternal sight,
to envision your life in the heart of God's will,
and to envision your new life that is born of Christ.

God Forever True

O, God forever true,
how much love have you,
enough to fill the ocean wide,
and stop the ebb and flow of tide,
enough to fill the starry skies,
the hosts of heaven would reply.

O, God forever true,
how much love have you,
you came to earth to die,
for a sinner such as I,
for me, you were love's sacrifice,
shed your life's blood in place of mine.

O, God forever true,
God of the universe are you,
time and space cannot equate,
nor the music of the sphere's placate,
 every cell, though they be minute,
by your Holy Spirit live and compute.

O, God forever true,
how much love have you,
how pleasant, O, how sweet,
to be in tune when 'ere we meet,
God in Christ and Christ in me,
your Holy Spirit's work complete.

God's Hand Decreed
Riding on the clouds,
driven by the four winds,
see the Son of God,
see the King of Kings,
following close behind,
the hosts of heaven are seen,
and the earth is shaken,
as the stars from heaven fall,
and all the graves are opened,
as all mankind bows low,
for every knee is weakened,
as the tidal waves begin to sweep,
over every man's hopes and dreams
'til all is covered by the dirt,
shattered by the debris,
And
to the world's renowned,
'tis God's hand that has decreed,
(as the four winds blow),
the tidal waves will not recede,
sparing neither man nor beast,
'til His anger is appeased.

God's Kingdom Come
In the pangs of destiny all plans of men do fly,
for all of life is born by God, born to live or to die,
the world's in the throes of agony as when a babe is born,
who fears beyond the safety that lies within it's mother's
womb,
but the world is in it's creators hand, no longer can any
man plan,
for in the pangs of it's new birth, there is a new heaven
and a new earth.

To believe God's Word or no,
for no other choice is at hand,
to enter God's Kingdom to come,
is all that is left for to plan,
man reached the point of no return,
many years ago in another time,
now, as then, one must decide,
wherein his heart his treasure lies.

God's Perfect Will
Oh Bright Light and Refining Fire,
Cleansing Agent and Pruning Pliers,
Holy Spirit of God, have your way,
for I must endure through all my days,

Oh penetrate the darkest place,
Oh Bright Light, to cleanse, erase,
and breathe on me, oh Refining Fire,
my vision be, and my desire,

Oh Guiding Light, be in my life,
go deeper 'til my soul is filled,
Oh Holy Spirit, my soul, be still,
that I may know your Perfect Will.

God's Truth Is Absolute
Red horses, black horses, ride with the wind,
patrol all the earth and report back again,
chariot wheels turn, white horses align,
dappled grays strain at the bit and the line,
Oh spirit's of fire, you are not for hire,
but to witness to God's Truth is your heart's desire,

Inward, out ward, all turn around,
as signature's signal the man about town,
Oh listen, be still, do you hear that sound,
the sound that echoes back to the distant drums,
for the devil roams the earth both to and fro,
for the devil seeks to destroy man's soul,

Hawks and eagles are circling low,
as life begets death's overflow,
now this old world's just a steppin' stone,
you can step up high or you can step down low,
to tell you the truth, the truth is absolute,
and the devil, it's true, doesn't have a clue,

Oh listen, be still, do you hear that sound,
the sound that beats louder than the distant drums,
there's a wolf among the sheep and he's bearing arms,
as signatures signal the beast renowned,
we must all turn around 'ere the last trumpet sounds,
perhaps yet God's Mercy and His Grace abound,

For 'tis the eleventh hour of the Spirit's Power,
'tis the outward sign of the inward mind,
'tis the seal of truth that needs no proof,
'tis the one last chance for the one last dance,
for in the twinkling of an eye,
then Jesus comes in Great Power,
but it is not for man to know the day or the hour,

Now I did not choose what went in this verse,
'cause a prophet speaks only what they have heard,
and if you think no prophets have been found,
just listen up close while the beat goes on,
do you know the truth that Jesus Christ has won,
and that the beat goes on 'til the day is done,

Yeah the beat goes on 'til the day is done
Oh, the beat goes on 'til the day is done.

God's Word in Jesus

The world is drowning in a sea of sorrow,
and all of creation gives place,
oh what, my God, what of tomorrow,
for all people have confusion of face,
all the knowledge of men has come to naught,
when knowledge and wisdom stand face to face,
the fear of the Lord is the wisdom not sought,
in God our Savior, the Prince of all Peace,
but words of wisdom are given to Him,
for by Him and through Him comes God's Grace,
and for those who seek God's Kingdom to come,
God's Word in Jesus, He does not forsake.

Impressions
Soft reflections on painted murals,
as artists notion to spark emotions,
bold impressions, sketches on papyrus,
displaying fears and revealing dreams,
in the iridescent lights of the painter's mind,
reflected on canvas one stroke at a time,
in panoramic paranoia, paranormal is redeemed.

Reflections
Raw emotions evoke devotions,
so loosen up, don't touch the cup,
the silver chalice in a man's palace,
leave the charger and the lager,
filled with extortion, with lust, and with greed,
the cup overflowing with rich man's creed,
they are all painted deserts without streams.

He's Coming Soon
All men will worship, all saints will sing,
glory in the highest, all praise to our King,
for soon Jesus is coming to earth once again,
Oh say, He is coming, sing again this refrain,

All men will worship, all saints will be raised,
in spirit and in truth, their hearts will all sing,
glory in the highest, all praise to our King,
for our Lord soon is coming, is coming again.

Holy Spirit Fresh and Sweet
What are these dry bones I see,
rising up from death's valley,
Oh breath of life, God calls to thee,
come breath of life into Christ's seed,
Oh valley of the souls at rest,
rise up to see, God sends His blest,
Oh hear the winds they call to thee,
'tis the Spirit of God that sets you free.

What is this great noise I hear,
'tis God's great army drawing near,
do not pause to cringe in fear,
for God has caused them to appear,
rise up assured in winged flight,
God's glorious angels will stand and fight,
as the battle din's left far behind,
o'er Satan's realm the sword comes down.

Thy way is blocked from going there,
Oh the vast graveyard, from sea to sea,
for God thy Savior has promised thee,
thy spirit shall live for eternity,
and thy soul shall be as an anthem sweet,
a song of praise sung for thy King,
where the saints and angels gather 'round,
all to praise our Lord, we are heaven bound.

Lightning flashes, thunder crashes,
around God's throne, a rainbow hastens,
and who are these from death set free,
with breath of life so fresh and sweet,
no more can Satan torment thee,
and no more bitterness can he mete,
the latter rains are past, are past,
fill up thy soul no more to fast.

Honey From The Rock
Oh taste and see that the Lord is good,
He leadeth me as He said He would,
when the days grow short and the nights are long,
the Lord is my Shepard, I shall not want,
Honey from the Rock, how sweet it is,
on my lips and on my tongue,
honey as sweet as the day is long,
in the cleft of the Rock, sweetest honey of all,
in the cleft of the Rock consecrated by God,
Oh my soul, on Him depend,
for my Advocate stands at God's right hand,
Oh my soul, rest assured in sleep,
be not dismayed where the river runs deep,
Jesus my Lord will give thee peace,
for where the Tree of Life and the river meet,
'tis there the children feast at God's Mercy Seat,
Oh honey from the Rock grant me strength once more
help me, Oh Lord, to carry on.

Hope
There is a rainbow,
'round God's Throne,
entreats the soul,
to look upon,
to see the glory,
of God's Son,
Oh shed the darkness,
of earth's core,
and leave behind,
earth's mantle torn,

There is a rainbow,
'round God's Throne,
entreats the spirit,
to follow home,
to see the glory,
of God's Son,
to leave behind,
what is no more,
to follow, follow,
when God calls.

How Does Your Garden Grow
Turn around, look behind you,
See what is there,
Little children are waiting,
Wondering if you care,
Turn around, look behind you,
Let your hearts beware,
Little children are suffering,
Because you're not there,
Turn around, look behind you,
Take time to care,
Little children who need you,
Too soon won't be there,
Turn around, look behind you,
See, God does care,
He weeps for the little children,
Whose daddy's aren't there,
Turn around, look behind you,
See what is there,
Little children now watching,
Look for someone else who cares!

1 Kings 13
Going home by another way,
the traveler stopped for awhile to stay,
but because he listened to a lie that day,
the traveler had his life to pay,

You may wander why, and so may I,
why one prophet died 'cause another one lied,
for he had listened to the voice of God,
and the prophet did as he was told,

But when he was tested along the way,
he ate and drank and so disobeyed,
for he harkened unto another voice that day,
when it was only God's voice he should have obeyed.

Imperfections

God did not make man imperfect,
man chose to be,
God did not create the world imperfect,
man caused it to be,
God did not cause men to hate,
man chose to hate,
God cannot live in the heart's of men,
who will not be reconciled to Him.

Lord, help me to love the unlovable,
for I am the unlovable,
Lord, help me to love the hated,
for I am the hated,
Lord, help me to love the imperfect,
for I am the imperfect,
for all of these I am,
though I have all the love of family and friends,
for all of these I am,
though I have eyes and ears and feet and hands,
for all of these I am,
each time I turn away from my fellow man.

In Disguise
A slice of the pie or castles in the sky,
none of these really matter when
one lays himself down to die,
the numbers six, sixty, six,
have been fixed, fixed, fixed,
in the heart of a man born
without a conscience,
a leading triage of total pretense,
in earth's midnight hour,
a heart's total eclipse,
when anarchy reigns,
and Death cold as ice,
leaving none to guess,
who's the man in disguise.

Inner Needs
We find it hard to comprehend,
that there is an inner need in man,
the need is there to give of oneself,
for the good of all mankind,
a need that lies dormant in each of us,
until the time, or times,
our spirit is wakened by our God,
who fills this void in our inner selves,
the spirit is wakened as if from deep sleep,
to complete the task that God has asked,
for all greatness attained by acts of men,
is the work of God's Spirit within,
filling the needs of the inner man.

Into The Light
On the sky-way to the stars,
on 'Jacob's Ladder' and beyond,
reaching out to claim life's crown,
no longer chained by fears, in bonds,
stretching psyche and with vision keen,
the future comes alive and it's promise is seen,
there on the skyway where God has deemed,
to fulfilling destiny, fulfilling dreams.

On the sky-way to the stars,
to where God's Promise can be grasped,
lunging toward a better world,
God meets us where time has elapsed,
for our spirit longs to soar even higher,
and to enter into that heavenly bliss,
while riding the sky-way to the stars,
entering into God's heavenly rest.

Beyond the sky-way, up into the stars,
to where the lightning flashes and the thunders clap,
to where the throne of God becomes the scene,
to where the stars bow low and the heaven depart,
to where the angels gather to loudly proclaim,
Oh Lamb of God forever crowned King,
the Glorious Light goes out from God's Throne,
becoming the Light for all mankind.

Israel's Birth-Right
Oh Love, what love, God's Pure Delight,
on wings of angels, shining bright,
the watchman cries, far gone the night,
Oh love of God, lead on forth-right,
for Israel's dream to overcome her plight,
yes, remove the veil and restore her sight,

With enraptured eye on God's Mercy Seat,
seeing the vision of the sparkling New Wine,
your new sensitivity procuring your rise,
you sing the new song for His Pure Delight,
yes, sing now, Oh Israel, beloved of Christ.
Oh Israel, see the glory of your birth-right.

Just a Pilgrim
Sometimes I'm so weary, I want to go home,
there is pain in my spirit and a longing in my soul,
for I want to see Jesus, the lover of my soul,
but He gives me strength e'er this body go.

Sometimes I'm so weary, there's a longing in my soul,
to be free form these shackles, only God doth know,
but on the other side of Jordan, there sets my goal,
a new body I'll be given and I will see my Lord.

Just A Seed

Some seed waft slowly on gentle summer breeze,
just to lay down their sleepy heads in the warmth of the sun,
while other seed is tossed by the wind and driven by the sea,
to be pierced in a far away land and covered by the shifting sand.

I am just a seed driven into the night,
driven there to choose between the wrong and the right,
I am just a seed gifted by God's light,
bearing witness for Him, to become more Christ-like,
I am just a seed pierced through and sighing,
note-worthy only because of Jesus Christ's dying,
I am just a seed carried into the night,
bearing witness to Him who is the Christ-Light.

Justified
Living on the edge of time,
the blood of Christ is the saints life-line,
they are sanctified with Christ to stand,
Oh covenant band, join hand in hand,

the light in the night that shines so bright,
in the circle of life see children of Christ,
they are working out salvations plan,
joined hand in hand, oh covenant band,

ever encircled by His Light,
living beyond the edge of time,
by the blood of Christ that justifies,
their candles burn forever bright.

Land of Unpleasantness
The aroma of sin is spread everywhere,
and the stench of sin permeates the very air,
the unholy aroma that God cannot bear,
rises up from the sinners lair,
though the animal kingdom be unaware,
the unrighteous mammon, God will not spare,
for the eyes of God see everywhere,
can one be found righteous when God is not near.

but when the Lion of Judah is seen in the air,
when Jehovah, our God, sends Him to tear,
at time of the harvest when the soul is laid bare,
woe upon woe for the heart ill prepared,
and woe is me if I'm caught unaware,
when God calls for His Righteousness to appear,
without which I am lost, sifted and laid bare
upon the threshing of the wheat, a seed of despair.

Oh Lord, may I be as thy maiden so fair,
dressed in white linen with her banquet prepared,
a pleasant aroma rising in the air,
the bride of Christ wearing jewels rare,
to the Immaculate Consummation,
of the virgin bride's sphere,
and may the bed of my affliction,
be stripped and laid bare,
Oh Lord, may I be as thy maiden so fair.

Letting Go
The sunflower bows,
it's head to pray,
as it's seeds drop into,
the cold, hard clay,
yet some it's seed,
the wind blows away,
as the sunflower bows,
it's head to pray,

May the seed find it's way,
through the cold, hard clay,
to feel the warmth of,
the bright sun's rays,
for surely God knows,
that some seeds blow away,
but only He knows,
which go and which stay,

Now as the sunflower bows,
it's head to pray,
so we too bow our heads,
and pray, God grant us,
strength for the long, hard day.

Life to Death to Life
Blood on sword, crown of thorns,
from life to death, the spirit gone,
sorrows deepened, souls orphaned,
sun eclipsed, night has come,
without God, without Son,

Resurrection morning comes,
God triumphant in God the Son,
affirmation, the battle won,
from death to life, the spirit's song,
God forever sits enthroned,
where myriads of angels,
surround the adored.

Life's Precious Balm
Into forgetfulness they throng,
leaving behind life's precious balm,
seeking release from their daily pain,
to a chemical repast souls become trained,
hungering, thirsting, but never filled,
seeking warmth from the daily chill.
desiring new life but new life never comes,
to the icy finger of death would many succumb,

What now, Oh Lord, Eternal God,
what now for these whose life was a song,
whose first only thought was just for the thrill,
who must face now the life that thou didst instill,
Lord keep us from ourselves we plead,
keep us from what our own eyes would seek,
for the life that seeks it's own to please,
must end in death's abstract poverty.

Lord, wouldst thou forgive, our sins atone,
that we may go and right the wrong,
to stand between, to plead thy cause,
to stand between, turn souls toward God,
Lord forgive what we have done,
judging and judging to thee belong,
true justice and mercy, let this be our song,
for you created all life, you are life's precious balm.

Love and Marriage

Love and marriage is - a dream, a trust and God's plan,
the giving and the accepting of love, side by side, hand in hand,
walking together through the trials of life, the sands of time to withstand,
in the giving and forgiving, the nature of love between a woman and a man
each one better because of the other, they are wonderfully, fearfully joined by God,
no longer to live as two, but one, the man and the woman consummated by love.

And the heart-felt pain caused by the one you love,
feels like being kissed by the thorns of the rose.

Love Only God

Love only one love,
Oh bride of Christ's longing,
because He first loved thee,

Love only one love,
the Christ of Calvary,
who died for you and me,

Love only one love,
Oh bride of Christ's longing,
He's coming to back for thee,

Love only one love,
for 'tis God in Christ you see,
who died to set us free.

Loved For Eternity

My Son, My Son,
the one I have loved,
loved with an everlasting love,
Hear, Oh Israel,
the Lord your God is One,
love the Lord your God,
with all your heart,
with all your mind,
and with all your strength,
Hear, Oh Israel,
the Lord is Elohim.

My son, my son,
the one I have loved,
loved with an everlasting love,
awake, Oh Israel,
awake, as if from deep sleep,
and look upon Him,
and mourn for Him,
as if for an only son,
yes, look upon Him,
the one who was pierced,
the one who himself is Elohim.

Man Cannot Be God

Man cannot be God because man cannot love as God loves,
Man cannot be God because man cannot forgive as God forgives,
True love is of God, lust is of man, man cannot be God,

the nature of God is Love,
the nature of man is lust,
man cannot be God.

At the height of ecstasy is the love of God,
but the depths of despair is to fear all alone,
let go of loneliness, fear of the unknown,
join in the chorus and sing along,
this truth is from God, His nature is Love.

Man's Quest

The quest of man is for to be,
released from his shackles, his spirit free,
freed from earth's mantle that binds, and then binds,
man-kind on his journey though space and time,
but no freedom from these shackles he finds,
for 'tis only Christ's Spirit through the ages of time,
that God gave to redeem the earth and man-kind,
to release the souls bound by space and by time.

Mene, Mene, Tekal, Parsin
One if by land, two if by sea,
what was the cost of our liberty,
was it paid for in blood,
was it paid for in pain,
was it paid for in the loss,
of our limbs, say the lame,
was it paid on the land,
was it paid on the sea,
was all paid in vain to
protect our liberty,
Three times then by land,
perhaps four times by sea,
and what of the fifth and sixth,
the seventh and the eighth,
without doubt, called by God,
Oh, the folly of man,
rolled up into one,
at what price then,
to purchase freedom.

My Heart's Desire

My heart's desire, Oh King of Kings,
is to be at home where the angels sing,
Oh heart's desire, I shall not weep,
as the bride of Christ, I'll be His queen,
so pure within, without, so sweet.

Oh with my Savior I'll soon meet,
to wed myself to Christ my King,
Oh heart's desire, what ecstasy,
pure within, without, so sweet,
to be one in heart my spirit sings,
in consummate with my God, my King

My Resting Place

Like a bird on the wing,
set free by her King,
as the winds lift me higher,
to His voice I aspire,
led by Devine Grace,
to find my resting place.

The winds carry me along,
in my heart there's a song,
I am His turtle dove,
and I'm flying toward home,
for it's by Devine Grace,
I'll find my resting place.

O, the song in my heart,
did Jesus impart,
now my portion of choice,
is to give Him my voice,
for 'twas by Devine Grace,
I found my resting place.

My Soul-Mate

My soul-mate, my true love, my friend,
my beloved, on whom my soul depends,
the one who is always quick to defend,
my hopes, my dreams, and all of my strength,
are built on the Rock of my defense,
in Jesus, my soul-mate, my true love, my friend.

Oh, For A Word From God

A golden dome, a silver chalice,
and a silver spoon inside a palace,
a dollar exchange, no peace, no quiet,
for a Word from God, no price can buy it.

A broken glass, a broken cistern,
for the bread of life many souls hunger,
a hardened soil where spirits lay quiet,
for the Word of God, how many passed by it?

One From Among Us

One from among us,
betrays with a kiss,
he is not for us,
his name is Judas,
born to exist,
but not to resist,
the one from among us,
who joins the anti-christ.

The one who walks among us,
who betrays with a kiss,
takes his leave of absence,
revealing his intent,
to join with the legions,
of the anti-christ,
to serve with his demons,
and not to repent.

One Lord
Lord,
You are one ,
and I am one,
make me one with Thee,
one in mind,
one in heart,
one in spirit with Thee,
Lord,
may it ever be.

Overturning
For reason of seasons,
believing is seeing,
yearning and learning,
about grieving and turning,
reflections and questions,
must lead to an ending,
lost love is not for retrieving,
but lost souls are for redeeming.

Slate cleared and waiting,
life is not for the fainting,
always challenging and changing,
but not of our understanding,
why the best gift we are given,
is the life we are living.

Paid In Full
Paid in full, just as I am,
paid in full by the blood of the lamb,
paid in full is the song of the saints,
paid in full, justified by faith,
vested in Christ's church, exemplified by it's works,
though across the wide valley lies many dry bones,
yet God is my witness, I am not alone,
not from this body, but a new life will come,
a brand new vessel with no sins to atone,
'tis the promise of God to carry me home.

Past The Gray Faux Pas
Past the gray faux pas of the Mardi Gras,
dressed in tresses, be it lads or lasses,

Let the throngs now pass, close up the gaps,
swing wide hell's gates, let the fires escape,
let the night be as light, let the wrong be as right,
to the souls that grasp, give them all they ask,
'til the tides recede to the ocean depths,
taking down the throngs that there entrenched,
enthralled by the seething sects,
in the coup de Grace of the Mardi Gras,

Be it lads or lasses in the shadow of death,
past the gray faux pas where the tides o'er swept.

Picture This
Lightning flashes, thunder crashes,
the boat is rocked by the stormy seas,
but down at the helm, Jesus sleeps,
a picture of God's Perfect Peace,

Jesus walks upon the waters,
as Peter sinks beneath the waves,
the hand of God reaches out to save,
the picture of God's Perfect Grace,

A bridge that spans the ocean depths,
a ship that sails o'er the gloomy mists,
a vision of eternal rest,
a picture time cannot erase,

No one can stop the wheels of time,
there is no riddle to this rhyme,
God creates both, the old and the new,
envision His eternal view.

Precious Living Water
Oh, most Gentle Father,
more precious than gold,
the Living Water,
poured out for my soul,
filling my heart to overflow.

Oh God, Holy Spirit,
Bright Morning Star,
more beautiful, more lovely,
most brilliant by far,
leaving thy imprint upon my heart.

Oh, Most Precious Father,
more precious than silver or gold,
who could deny you created all life,
sealed with your promise,
to fill each heart to overflow.

Pride of Life
From her crystal palace,
flying swiftly to his aide,
the bride of Satan follows,
where the pride of life would lead,
vying to inspirit, vying to enslave,
the souls whom Christ would save,

Attempting always to usurp,
the authority of God's Word,
the pride of life is ever,
the bane of all the earth,
while from her crystal palace,
she accomplishes the devil's work.

Rivers of Tears
Rivers of tears flow down from the throne,
from the throne of our God Most High,
but the Lamb of God, in utterances unknown,
in groans that shake the foundations of earth and sky,
intercedes for His flock as He stands alone,
before the throne of our God Most High,
and rivers of tears flow down from the throne,
as God blesses the flock through the blood of Christ.

Saving Grace
O, I can save face,
because of God's grace,
he helps me to stand,
on the rock, not the sand,
yes, I can save face,
because of God's grace,
because Jesus came to save---
because Jesus came to save.

O, my heart has been changed,
'ere since Jesus came,
for He died in place,
to save me from my fate,
from my sins I've been cleansed,
have assurance within,
because Jesus came to save--
because Jesus came to save.

O, it's all in God's plan,
He's the Great 'I Am',
He says call on me,
and I'll set you free,
on the Rock you will stand,
held firm by His hand,
because Jesus came to save---
because Jesus came to save.

Signed and Sealed
Signed, sealed, and delivered,
or branded and led to the slaughter,
sealed by the hand of Almighty God,
or marked by the hand of Lucifer,
"Who is the owner of your soul?"

To become like Christ, Lord of all,
run, not walk, away from strife,
tell all the world whose side your on,
let your heart be circumcised,
by the all-sufficient, El Elyon

Somebody's Knocking
Somebody's knockin', won't you let Him come in,
Someone is pleading, Oh, please let Him come in,

'tis Jesus who's knockin', won't you open the door,
let Him come in and you'll live forever more,

Oh see how He weeps as He walks away,
for the door did not open to Jesus today,

Somebody's knockin', somebody's knockin',

maybe tomorrow, He won't be turned away,
Oh, that tomorrow will not be too late.

Somebody's knockin', somebody's knockin'.

Son of Righteousness
Come out from among them, I say,
no longer do I send you away,
my children, I am coming to save,
the Son of Righteousness, I send today,

Come out from among them, I say,
no longer be fearful or afraid,
'tis the promise of God, stand in faith,
behold, Jesus comes at the end of the age,

God calls to His children, come home,
redeemed of the faith, sins atoned,
gathered by angels, the saints 'round His Throne,
praise God forever in your heavenly home.

Spirit to Spirit
Spirit to Spirit,
my heart is delivered,
by Jesus, my Savior,
forever and ever,

He opened my heart,
to receive circumcision,
and my soul is delivered,
by my Redeemer/Kinsman,

Spirit to Spirit,
caught up to heaven,
I'll be with my Savior,
forever and ever.

Star-Bursts

Star-bursts of light from the sun's flaming orb,
feed the dying embers of planet earth's final hour
open fissures form where the fires erupt,
throughout the earth's fragile crust,
the star-bursts of light fade into the night,
and darkness prevails for the heavens are not.

Though the earth pass away in a flash, out of sight,
and the darkness prevails o'er the souls damned in flight,
there remains to be seen the everlasting light,
though the earth pass away with a terrible noise,
up in the clouds a new earth is poised,
to fill up the void where the old is no more.

A new earth is planted, and a new heaven,
there remains God in Christ, the everlasting light,
and His bride in her glory is more than a dream,
there's a new song in heaven, saints and angels sing,
O' beautiful Savior, how sweet the refrain,
all glory, all honor is due Jesus' name.

The Art of Giving
The art of giving lies,
in the pouring out of self,
given over to the service of God,
to the ultimate, unfathomable life,
redeemed by the gift borne of sorrow,
at the pinnacle of his life all alone stands love.

The Bride In The Mists
Who is this kissed by the mists,
running to and fro, looking for the blest
for the promise sealed, would time stand still,
for the lilies field, would the mountains shield,
for the bride's trousseau, would the groom e'er yield,
to be kissed by the mists, would the heavens reel,

Who is this standing in the mists,
'neath the bridal veil waiting to be sealed,
would the bride-groom meld to the bride he shields,
and would time stand still, would the heavens yield,
would the sun and the moon and the stars be felled,
would the veil e'er lift o'er the bride in the mists.

The Crown Jewels
We are to Him as precious jewels,
so different side by side, and yet,
the same, as each facet of our being,
reflects the brilliance of His light,
we are turned and perfected by His hand,
we are the crown jewels of the Prince,
cut and polished by the Master's plan,
prepared for the coronation of the King of Kings,
reflecting His Light from within, without,
different as we are, side by side,
in His Spirit we are His chosen Bride,
created in His Image, the children of light.

The Deep, Dark Abyss
In the dark of night,
the lights shine bright,
on the senses dulled,
by sins promised delights,
on the flag unfurled,
to the tune of the world,
to the dirt and the grime,
on it's silver and pearls,
on hell's mouth agape,
to receive men's pay,
for in the dark of night,
no one can escape,
the deep, dark abyss,
made to separate,
man's sin and his blight,
from God's Pure Light.

In The Eternal God-Light
Turning and turning, driven out of sight,
the tip of the auger draws the seed close behind,
spiraling downward until the time is right,
'til the new dawn breaks forth in it's glorious light,
'til from out of death's darkness, O what a beautiful sight,
comes the heart of the flower, the star shining bright,
unfolding, spirit yielding and to it's pure delight,
spiraling upward, heralding it's new life,
on the wings of God's Love, carried to new heights,
melded and molded by the Eternal God-Light.

The Fiery Furnace
Into the fiery furnace,
ride the six hundred, the sixty and six,
demon squadrons of the millennium,
flying into the devil's pit,
as heavy smoke belches out,
from where the earth is split,
and the stench of death rises,
from the ashes that stood for,
the six hundred and sixty-six.

But multitudes and multitudes,
join in the heavenly chorus,
souls delivered from the flaming torches,
kindled by the fire of God's wrath,
projected in violent fashion,
against the world, the arrogant masses,
who bear the marked resemblance,
of the beast and of his image,
until the sword of the Lord is sated,
see, the Day of the Lord advances.

The Gift

I am a poet though I did not know it,
'twas a gift from God, but He could not bestow it,
He told me to wait but I hastened away,
He asked me to listen, but I was afraid,
for I choose to go my own sinful way,
doing my own thing through all my days,
now my message is this, if to God you request,
then wait 'til He answers, His gifts are best.

The Great Eagle

The great eagle lifts his mighty wings,
intent to survey the wide sweeping plains,
through the clouds he plummets,
to destroy without thought,
to grasp and to choke,
his great talons close tight,
the leopard, the bear,
they too, are there,
and the roaring lion,
who prowls to and fro,
ripping and tearing,
wherever he goes,
in his blood-drenched robe,
that old serpent of old,
wreaks havoc and vengeance,
upon men's souls,
but the islands retreat,
the mountains tremble in fear,
as THE LORD in all His Glory,
Suddenly Appears.

The House of Cards
See it tumble, see it fall, the house of cards built up so tall,
fabrication on flimsy walls,
white-washed over, the house of cards,
and the infamous character of the joker's wild,
embraces the face of the devil's child,
'til up from the smoke, from the cinders arise,
the great escapade of the anti-Christ,

O' see it tumble, see it fall, the great, the mighty, Babylon's moll,
the inflated character of blood and guns,
white-washed over and shunned by God,
the serpent that slithers up the new mud-run,
while across the sun his demons lunge,
O' beware of the beast as the great succumb,

O' see it tumble, see it fall, hear now the cries from Babylon,
O' house of cards built up on lust,
smoke curls now `round your candle snuffed,
the joker's wild falls on his face and the devil's child finds no more place,
O' house of cards fallen to disgrace, lick now the dust from hell's fire grate,
O' listen, listen, leave post-haste, for the fiery furnace lets none escape,
O' house of cards, why are you praised,
in the time of testing you are disgraced,
and in the day of judgment there is no debate,

the BLOOD OF CHRIST IS ALL THAT SAVES,
O' beware of the time, the end of the age,
see, Christ comes to seal your fate.

The Iron and The Clay
Wedged in between,
and pinned in tight,
the clay begins to tremble,
something isn't right,
for when iron strikes iron,
the sparks ignite.

O, man of clay,
it's mirrored in your eyes,
you know you're just the pawn,
of an elusive goliath.

The Man In The Blue Silk Suit
See the man in the blue silk suit,
his works are revealed in the light of the truth.

He's the man with the plan to enrich the land,
and the silver that jingles in his pockets,
is for buying time, though he cares not for it,
his deepest thought is for the power he covets,
and he's seeking to cancel out all of his debits,
from the highest place, the seat of the president.

See the man in the blue silk suit,
his works are revealed in the light of the truth.

The Meeting Place
I'll love you forever,
Oh, heart of my heart,
tho' one heart remain,
while the other departs,
forgiving, forgiven,
to you I'll be true,
accepting God's Truth,
to believe in Christ too,

Tho' one should remain,
while the other departs,
transformed, now transplanted,
into that heavenly blue,
but, Oh heart of my heart,
we'll dance again to love's tune,
at God's meeting place,
in the heavenly blue.

The Memorial Seed
The memorial seed is planted,
but the fruit of the seed is yet to be seen,
will thorns and thistles there grow,
or the fruit of the spirit so sweet,
and what shall we then say of the morrow,
we shall say fear God and learn from our sorrow,
for the answers we seek are not buried shallow,
but lie deep in the spirit where Christ is hallowed.

The Nature of The Beast
The nature of the beast at work,
world government doing it's worst,
with nothing left to be declared,
world taxing has left the table bare,
no crumbs to fall beneath our feet,
faces are pale and taunt with grief,
last meals are eaten in bitter sorrow,
no hope is left, none for tomorrow,
no one is left to mind the store,
and no one is left to govern o'er,

Kings of the earth sit in the dust,
their nostrils fill, their breathing stops,
whose vision was, oh this horror unknown,
now they must reap what they have sown,
they feared not God, nor regarded any man,
they filled their plates and struck up the band,
they worshiped gods of brick and stone,
exchanging life for silver and gold,

Theirs was the nature of the beast at work,
but they have earned their full reward,
look up oh denizens from thy perch,
for where ever the eagles gather to watch,
the sun beats down in relentless mirth,
and the north winds blow their chilling blast,
oh desert sands swirl 'round, give birth,
to the end of life on planet earth.

The Old, Old Story
Here's the story, learn it well
rejecting God, the angel fell.

And a tree grew tall with leafy boughs,
for the tree was planted there by God,
yet the axe was wielded and the tree was felled,
though his limbs spread out to shelter all,

Here's the story, learn it well,
a tree grew tall above his fellows,
for his seed was sown where the soil was fallowed,
his roots grew deep, his roots grew strong,
but denying God, the tree grew proud,
so he was torn out, roots and all.

Here's the story, learn it well,
beneath the tree grew up a vine,
o'er the fertile land he spread his lineage,
breaching walls and sipping vintage,
promising much, but producing little,
the vine soon learned to speak in riddles,
and the vine forgot, God was his creator,
and so the pride of the vine became dry and brittle.

And the lion roared, and the lion tore,
still he was snared where he was born,
and the eagle's wings lift him no more,
his pride deflated, he has grown old,
no one can help, there are no allies,

and because he left his own first love,
no one is left to hear his mournful sighs,
still rejecting God, the eagle dies.

Here's the story as old as time,
the God of old who makes things known,
He who lifts up nations or tears them down,
is the same today as yesterday,
and the same tomorrow, when the new day dawns,
O, heed the lessons, give to God prime-time,
ask Him to bless and to multiply,
the fruit of your labor in the name of Christ.

The Open Door
The open door, the heart of home,
the place of rest, the souls abode,
the peaceful valley, the sun above,
all anchored in place by the Lord of Love,

Scarred hands beseech, that all may know,
God's Shepherd leads to the open door.

Trust and obey, my only need,
refreshing Spirit, to rest in thee,
Oh Shepherd lead, thy way I seek,
to know thy love is perfect peace.

Satan, The Religious Demagogue
In staged and disciplined fright,
and with extraordinary might,
derived from the senses of sound and sight,
Appolyon of Sheol deceives many souls,

With demonic fires burning bright,
the moon is held captive in his sight,
by the fires that blot out the starry night,
as Appolyon of Sheol takes captive many a soul.

Truth is not found in the dark of the night,
where the transients looking to the stars,
number the blows aimed at our God,
as Appolyon of Sheol laughs uncontrolled.

But Jehovah is God and Jesus is King,
with truth as His banner, the Son of God reigns,
to Him be all glory, to Him be all praise,
for Appolyon of Sheol lies defeated and slain.

To God be all glory, to Him be all praise,
for Jehovah is God and Jesus is King
where is thy victory, O' death, where thy sting,
as for Appolyon of Sheol, regard no more his name.

The Rocks Cry Out
The rocks cry out,
from beneath the earth,
the rocks cry out,
as a witness to truth,
inscriptions written,
by the hand of man,
are uncovered now,
by the shifting sands,

Oh the rocks cry out,
that the prophets are slain,
that the weak die young,
because anarchy reigns,
Oh the rocks cry out,
let it be known,
that men are crushed,
beneath their heavy loads,
to return to the dust,
from which they were hewn,
to be judged by God,
the rock that hones.

The Safe Harbor

What light from yonder lighthouse beams,
what light searches out the depths of life's sea,
what light offers hope to the great ship in need,
nearing death's cavern 'neath the breaking waves.
as the earth spins around, it is to God's rhythm,
for all things must end, e'en the earth has it's season,
God has placed here a watchtower that can' be denied,
and from His throne in glory He judges mankind.

Oh what light from yonder lighthouse beams,
as the earth spins around the light can be seen,
beckoning the ship while there is yet time,
anchor in the safe harbor, hold fast the life-line.

The Scars You Bear

Oh brother of mine, why do you swear,
what terror lurks 'neath the mask you wear,
could it be what you have seen,
a specter of the most sinister dare,

Oh brother mine, why do you swear,
could it be the horror seen there,
of the specter with a rapist flair,
attacking your sister within his lair,

Oh brother mine, do no more swear,
for we are saved as God draws near,
He draws us into His greater sphere,
for God knows all the scars you bear.

The Seven Spirits of God
The seventh day, creation finite,
the seventh night, a paradigm,

The 7 Spirits of our God,
the 7th word heard from the cross,

The 7th seal, let it be known,
the angels gather 'round God's Throne,
and the living creatures and the throngs,
holy, holy, holy, they all chant enthralled.

The 7th king in transition,
the 7th of his generation,
the 7th trumpet, creation groans,
the seven bowls to earth are thrown.

The 7th year ends Jacob's plight,
and the 7th heaven is paradise.

The Ultimate Word

In the game of life,
when all the numbers are told,
both providence and destiny,
tell all the world that God's in control,

He is the first, He is the last,
His Life is the ultimate Word,
and when all the world begins to groan,
He's the only one who stands alone,

He's the Son of God, the Anointed One,
He is Jesus Christ, Redeemer/Kinsman,
He is King of Kings and Lord of Lords,
He is GOD Most High, The Three-in-One,

The Unseen Power

The unseen power of the sower,
is the knowing in the gloaming,
that the Word of God, the Heart of God,
waters the soil where the sower toils,
'til the unseen power gives life to the seed,
producing the harvest of the redeemed.

The Well-Spring of Life
From out of the wilderness,
Through great suffering and death,
The Well-Spring of life,
Breaks open the depths,
While the tree in the garden,
Was removed roots and all,
Stripped of it's branches,
And left to dry out,
Now the spirits below,
Ask what does this all mean,
That the Son of God,
Should come down from His Throne,
To walk among men,
And to die for them all,
So let all take note,
That through His suffering and death,
The Well-Spring of life,
Has broken open the depths.

There Is Light
Is the valley low, do you feel forsaken,
is your strength zapped, has your faith been shaken,
and does Satan tell you that God doesn't listen,
does he make you feel that death soon hastens,
remember that life has it's high and it's lows,
you may pricked by a thorn when you pick a rose,
just remember God's promise, by His Grace there is light,
and from His throne flows freely the river of life,
He is the hope eternal in the darkest night,
He is strength for the weary, He makes all things right,
God will not forsake nor will He forget,
you can rest in His Love and in His Peace Perfect.

Thus Sayeth The Lord
Not by power nor by might, thus sayeth the Lord,
but by the very words that proceed from thy mouth,
thy Spirit poured out in the days of the latter rains,
Oh God, be the judge, the judge of all men.

Time-Lines
Don't drop,
through the top,
through the mantle,
into the channel,
snatch from the fire,
by strong desire,
listen up, fill the cup,
to the overflow of the soul,

Don't drop,
from the top,
through strong desire,
be prayerful criers,
for the channel is deep,
where the soul doth sleep,
and the Word in Truth,
is the God Triune.

Time-Slots
Today is…
tomorrow is not,
yesterday is emptied,
of it's time-slot,
Today is…
the hour at hand,
the time allotted,
to the sons of man,
Today is…
the grim reaper awaits,
'tis the hour of judgement,
that all men must face,
Today is…
tomorrow is not,
eternity beckons,
no more time-slots.

To Share a Blessing
To all who have seen, to all who may ask,
it seems odd that God has blessed me with this task,
but all blessings flow down from God's heavenly throne,
and to all who receive it, God has a plan,
to tell all the world what He has done.

Total Abandon

Given over to abandon,
every law and every standard,
the world is destined to be shaken,
for God who judges will not pardon,
be alert, be awake to abominations,
and catastrophic desolations,
for God has called Christ to action,
your souls are saved by your patience,

White-washed walls and demagogues,
armored tanks and Santa Claus,
ivory palaces and movie stars,
move the world to stand in awe,
win or lose, we gamble all,
'til in death, the curtains fall,
removing traces of all races,
all must return to dust and ashes.

Turning Point
What has man to do with God,
when man thinks he needs no one,
what has man to do with God,
when God's Spirit has abandoned,
what has man to live then for,
when God to him has closed the door,
what hope has man to be like his God,
when his spirit from him has flown,

Turn, Turn, Turn,
why, Oh man, will you not learn,
why, Oh man, will you not turn,
why, Oh man, will you yet die,
without hope, and without God,
why, oh man, must your soul burn,
gnashing, weeping, never sleeping,
turn to God, find your way home.

Two Hearts, Far Apart
Black heart's placard,
the slogan of the dragon,
destroy God's Kingdom,

Brave heart, True heart,
the Word of God, never wrong,
the First, the Last, always God,
listen to the Victor's song,

Two heat's far apart,
can never, ever together come.

Walking In The Fire

Walking in the fire,
hungering for the Spirit's Power,
snatched from death,
in the earth's final hour,
investing ourselves,
in the body of Christ,
many are walking,
through the fire,
hungering for the Spirit's Power,
witnesses to His higher calling.

When The Reapers Come

The tree is topped,
it's growth has ended,
it's ready for the reapers,
for God will send them,
and when the tree is felled,
when man-kinds shelter is gone,
God's angels will gather the harvest,
when the reapers come.

Wisdom vs. Riches
Money speaks,
but reality boasts,
the four winds blow it,
from coast to coast,
lessons are learned,
but never are sought,
(time is lost,
O, count the cost),
yet by God's Spirit,
we all are taught,
Holy Spirit,
grace our lives,
and lead us on,
to Paradise.

Y2K
Two kilos,
two philos,
two kings,
of one mind,
blood mingled,
heart's single,
two vines,
enter-twined,
a king's ransom,
for a nation,
but do not mention,
superstition,
With too little,
too late,
many stand,
at the gates,
words of knowledge,
not to suffice,
not by works,
but by God's grace,
little earned,
nothing gained,
no Agape Love,
forgiveness disdained,
and now blood mingles,
with the flames.

A Growing Faith
People come and people go,
but God is constant and remains,
to shore up the waters and break the waves.

Fear not for the days at hand,
for God is always in command,
the times shall pass, you will soon see,
these days have made your faith grow deep.

The days of sunshine will return,
then you'll look back on what you've learned,
'tis God's hand that caused you to stand firm,
for 'tis by God's hand the tides are turned.

Golden Apples
Golden apples, filling treats
juicy morsels, tidbits sweet,
inner secretions can't help but speak,
of those golden apples, those healthy treats.

Freda V. Lieb

Growing Beyond
From a place somewhere inside us,
from a place where no one can return,
there is a child to remind us,
to accept what we all must learn,
the child remain steadfast and sure,
of the courage it takes to grow beyond,
and yearns for a place to call his own,
understanding that no one can go alone.

Inspiration Point
Easter Bonnets,
and silly sonnets,
ribbons and bows,
all for show,

Frilly dresses,
curly tresses,
shining faces,
on lads and lasses,

Sun on horizon,
Easter lesson,
learn the reason,
Christ has risen.

Down A Winding Dirt Road

Do you know the little girl who lived down the road,
She had curly pig-tails and a turned-up nose,
And she lived next door to the old woman in the shoe,
I must ask her about a thing, or, maybe two,

Do you know the little girl who lived down the road,
With her curly pig-tails and her worn-out shoes,
See, she walks a long way down the winding dirt road,
And I must ask her a thing, or, maybe two,

Am I the little girl who lived down the road,
With her curly pig-tails frozen in the cold snow,
With frost-bite on her fingers and tears in her clothes,
For I have walked a long way down a winding dirt road.

How Now, The Spotted Cow

How now, the spotted cow,
the duck runs amuck at the cat's meow,
the freaked out dog howls at the moon,
'cause the monkey just rattled his bone.

How now, the spotted cow,
the fungus among us spews out his brew,
while the little girls pout and the little boys shout,
and the monkey, well I guess he just missed his cue.

How now, holy cow,
how did you jump over that moon,
the pie in the sky pokes your good right eye,
as you fall back to earth, now good night.

Over The Hill with Jack and Jill

Jack and Jill went up the hill,
guess what they went after,
Jack fell down and broke his crown,
but Jill broke into laughter,

Locate the moral to my story and you will be the wiser,
expect disappointments, expect long delays,
that the rip-tide will suck strong men to their graves,
but when good times come, will you be surprised,
for the best things in life one always must wait.

The Ring Of Gold

Ride a painted pony, walk a narrow street,
the thrill is in the victory, but Oh the agony of defeat,
Listen to the music, can you hear the beat,
the angels all are singing an anthem oh so sweet,

You ride the painted pony across a muddy stream,
walk up a crooked holler, so glad you made it home,
and you listen to the music as the church bells ring,
they tell the old, old, story, you are so glad you came,

Oh listen to the music as the children bid you come,
come ride the painted pony but the golden ring is gone,
still you ride the painted pony though it cannot make a
sound,
and you can hear the music as the pony goes around,

So ride the painted pony, watch as dreams go by,
as they fade into the glory of God's painted sky,
and listen to the music as dreamers often do,
it's not so much the words they sing, it's the beat you
listen to,

Ride on the painted pony until your life is gone,
it can only take you back again to right where you got on,
Oh listen, hear the music, the beat goes on and on,
it's telling you a story, the ring of gold has none,

Yes listen to the music, maybe write a country song,
then teach the little children how to sing along,
as you ride the painted pony across a muddy stream,
walk up a crooked holler 'til at last you make it home.

Raising Lions Brave

Little boy, little boy, why are you so blue,
didn't mama teach how to tie your shoes,
papa didn't raise you on a playground for fools.

Little boy, little boy, why do you run away,
be like the lion who knows he is dyin',
and that's why he stalks his prey.

Little boy, little boy, why stand there in the gloom,
didn't papa raise you to stand up brave and true,
and mama didn't raise you to be the lions food.

Little boy, little boy, be like the lion unafraid,
stand up tall against the wrong,
and let your conscience lead the way.

The Little Brave and The Little Maiden

The little brave wears his eagle plumage
and the little maiden wears hers braids,
together they scale
the mountain-top high,
as swift as the eagles
that soar in the sky,
together they cross
the hot desert sand,
come to the Living Water
in the Promised Land,
and now when ever they go out to play,

the little brave wears his eagle plumage,
and the little maiden wears her braids,
how else can the little brave,
carry his fair maiden away.

The Looking Glass Re-Visited
Falling through the cracks into the looking glass,
now would you look at that, it seems that Alice is back,
with scissors in hand, forget about plans,
cut through the grime, become Alice's mime,
falling through the cracks is such a simple task,
just drop into the abyss of the looking glass,
for to live in the past is to ask, then to ask,
why must we remiss our days filled with regrets,
and ne'er again bring to task the years of youthful bliss,
must we drop though the cracks of our own looking glass,
to look into the abyss to see what we've missed,
for the time to repair flies by as we stare,
at the naked truth reflected on the face in the mirror.

The Hiding Place Lost
Behind closed doors, hiding in a closet,
a child has found a haven when she feels neglected,
but then the doors are locked and her haven lost,
the hiding place reveals a child that is molested,
violated and bereaving, the child just lays there weeping,
for when the doors were locked her hiding place was lost.

In the hiding place there a scene unfolds,
in the form of a man and a child just three years old,
seeking and relentless his hands tear at her clothes,
and he steals away her innocence there behind closed doors,
while in the hiding place lost, he threatens and he scolds,
and believing all his lies the child does as she is told.

How many years were spent locked behind closed doors,
ravaged and tormented by all the lies that she was told,
how many tears are spent before the child grows bold,
and from the hiding place reveals the lies that scarred her soul,
though it once was her safe haven, that hiding place of old,
filled with child-hood memories, they are lost forever more.

Wisdom Speaks
He held you in his arms
and he kissed you,
he told you how much he
had missed you,
for a brief encounter,
he deferred,
and then he returned,
to her,
'trust me' with his mouth,
he touts,
but trustworthy he is found,
to be not,
true love is the treasure,
to find,
when the past is left,
far behind.

Freda V. Lieb

Success
Of God in Christ,
yearn to learn,
to speak your need,
and let Him lead,

Blue on blue,
time on time,
all in all,
done and done,

Win on win,
trey success,
move on truth,
pass the test.

Kathy Ann's Blessing
Kathy Ann runs, chasing the wind,
but God's Love surrounds her changing all her plans,
for God has in mind a life hid in Christ,
and a home eternal in the circle of life,
so be still, if you will, and stand in your place,
be still, if you will, to receive God's grace,
for God's Spirit surrounds you, He calls you by name,
And the four winds echo the song of His praise,
find your heart's desire by trusting in Him,
for God's Spirit calls to you from within, from within,
now Kathy Ann run, and let your heart be content,
your future is secure for Gad has it all planned.

Larry E's Blessing

Larry E, Larry E, you've a zest for life,
but a life at its best is full of trouble and strife,
yet God has a plan to make all things new,
for the glory of His name, He has sanctified you,
(His promise is sure, His word is true),
and God has a plan to increase and expand,
for little is much when it's placed in God's hand,
now His Cleansing Spirit sweeps away the debris,
of all trouble and strife as the Son sets you free,
so do not despise small beginnings in Christ,
for He is the capstone in the building of life,
taken under His wing, covered by His Love,
in the new life He gives, you've a new zest for God,
as the power of God fills you, and His Spirit of Truth,
the Glory of Christ will surround all you do.

Phillip Jon's Blessing
Phillip Jon struggles,
against the wind,
seeking release,
from the turmoil within,
Oh let the winds carry you,
lift your eyes to the sky,
let the four winds carry you,
to your heart's desire,
see God's Spirit descends,
on you like a dove,
to give you His Grace,
to bring you His Love,
Oh let the four winds,
carry you aloft,
for God gives you His Word,
the four winds to calm,
and wisdom to speak,
in tongues from above,
that you may spread abroad,
the gift of His Love,
in the precious anointing,
of His tender touch,
because of god Grace.

Draw close now to Him,
knowing full well, His passion to indwell,
the chosen seed of Israel,
and you, His precious child,

Freda V. Lieb

you are Christ's seed through His sufferings,
and through His Triumphant Power,
by His Grace sanctified unto glory.

Tony G's Blessing
Tony G, Tony G, busy as a bee,
but the bee turns to sting you, to bring you grief,
yet God's in control and He has other plans,
for the bee lost its sting in a faraway land,
determined by God and told beforehand,
now wisdom and knowledge and all God's Precepts,
all the gifts of His Spirit that are given without cost,
are to well up within you as a balm for you soul,
and for His Kingdom, that you also may know,
His Spirit of compassion that knows no bounds,
and the passion of His Love for you as His son,
for the bee has no power against God's higher call,
and love's light still shines bright in the middle of the
night,
when the bridegroom returns to claim His pure bride.

Freda V. Lieb

Treasures In My Home
Top Hat in my lap,
candy kisses for my favors,
enter castles, though not on paper,
stepping up to meet new faces,
(but fame and fortune,
in heaven's light,
dim the stars personified),

Listen while I tell my story,
how God has blessed me by His Mercy,
on my left and on my right,
run little children of the light,
spreading out in all directions,
treasures of my home and heavens'
tender hearts on beaming faces,
shining bright stars for Jesus.